DATE LOANED

Dec 9 '57 M

INGLIS LECTURES
IN SECONDARY EDUCATION

Trends in American Secondary Education. By Leonard V. Koos. 1925.

Opportunity and Accomplishment in Secondary Education. By Paul H. Hanus. 1926.

OPPORTUNITY
AND ACCOMPLISHMENT
IN SECONDARY EDUCATION

LONDON : HUMPHREY MILFORD
OXFORD UNIVERSITY PRESS

The Inglis Lecture, 1926

OPPORTUNITY
AND ACCOMPLISHMENT
IN SECONDARY EDUCATION

BY

PAUL H. HANUS

CAMBRIDGE

HARVARD UNIVERSITY PRESS

1926

COPYRIGHT, 1926
BY HARVARD UNIVERSITY PRESS

PRINTED AT THE HARVARD UNIVERSITY PRESS
CAMBRIDGE, MASS., U.S.A.

THE
INGLIS LECTURESHIP

To honor the memory of Alexander Inglis, 1879–1924, his friends and colleagues gave to the Graduate School of Education, Harvard University, a fund for the maintenance of a Lectureship in Secondary Education. To the study of problems in this field Professor Inglis devoted his professional career, leaving as a precious heritage to his co-workers the example of his industry, intellectual integrity, human sympathy, and social vision. It is the purpose of the Lectureship to perpetuate the spirit of his labors and contribute to the solution of problems in the field of his interest. The lectures on this foundation are published annually by the School.

FOREWORD

TWO reasons impelled me to accept the invitation of the Committee in charge of the Inglis lecture in Secondary Education to deliver the lecture this year.

My first reason is found in the tribute of Dean Holmes to Professor Inglis at the memorial exercises in honor of Professor Inglis in May, 1924. Dean Holmes said: "The sense of our personal loss must indeed be heavy upon us; but we are gathered here to express our confidence that the work he did was significant, and to confess our obligation to carry it on." And again: "Let us determine to devote ourselves, in the broad unselfish spirit in which he worked, to the solution of educational problems, and to the building of a science and phi-

FOREWORD

losophy of education upon foundations unshakable."

Although not a specialist in secondary education, I was glad to attempt, however imperfectly, "to carry on" in the sense given to those words by Dean Holmes.

My second reason is this. In attempting to contribute my bit to the work which death prevented Inglis from carrying on, I feel myself, once more, associated with my friend and colleague in the work which we both loved, and in which he led.

P. H. H.

OPPORTUNITY
AND ACCOMPLISHMENT
IN SECONDARY EDUCATION

IT IS FAIR to say, I think, that the endeavor to improve our secondary education has been and is most marked in the public-high-school field; although it has not been confined to that field, and in quite recent times some of the most significant endeavor has taken place in private and endowed schools.

To present in outline — and I shall not attempt to do more — certain agencies and the procedures which have functioned in bringing our contemporary opportunity for secondary education to its present stage of development, I shall have to traverse ground that I know is, or has been, familiar to many of you. I give a brief account of these agencies and procedures, nevertheless, because it is essential to my present purpose to do so, because I know that people — even teachers — forget, and because they illustrate a fruitful method of solving educational problems — a method which, so far as I know is the peculiar invention of this country. I mean the method of voluntary cooperation. I shall have occasion to refer to this method again, later on.

Because our secondary schools originated as college preparatory schools, and because a practice once established tends to perpetuate itself, — becomes conventionalized,— college admission requirements continued to determine the aims and scope of the work of secondary schools for many years. When the academies entered the field, that aim was an essential feature of their total aim. If it had not been, the academies would have failed to meet the demands

SECONDARY EDUCATION

of an important part of their constituency. In time, that aim has overtopped all other aims in most of the academies that have survived the competition with the public high schools. It is, of course, normally and desirably, a persistent aim of the public high schools of today. In the best high schools, or city systems of high schools, it neither obscures the aims of the schools as independent educational institutions serving the varied educational needs of their respective communities, nor interferes with them. In many less favorably circumstanced high schools, however, — a large proportion of the total number, — the college preparatory aim is still dominant enough to ensure the lion's share of the total educational offering of those schools; or at least, to influence profoundly the aims, scope, and methods of all the work, even when, as sometimes happens, the college admission requirements reflect aims and methods at variance with or antagonistic to the independent functions of the high schools as community schools.

It may seem anomalous, at first sight, that the college preparatory aim should still be as influential as it is in public high schools sending few or no pupils to college, since that aim was the chief cause of the decline of public interest in the publicly supported secondary schools during the eighteenth century and part of the nineteenth. But the reason for this seeming anomaly is not far to seek. Apart from the fact that college admission requirements are no longer restricted to little more than Latin and Greek, it was and is universally recognized that college-preparatory pupils belong, for the most part, to the leading classes of society — the fortunate and influential classes. Such members of society are known to possess a degree of education, or at least an appre-

SECONDARY EDUCATION

ciation of it, which the other members of society do not possess, and to which, in large part, they attribute their more fortunate economic and social position. Ambitious persons who are not yet members of the leading classes may and do cherish the ambition to attain the economic independence and social influence of those classes through education. Accordingly, the college preparatory work, affording, as it does, the education sought by the leading classes, has always enjoyed and still enjoys a social distinction not possessed by the other work of the schools. Moreover, discerning parents were and are aware that the work not included in, or not accepted for, college admission by the colleges was, and sometimes still is, inferior in thoroughness to the college-preparatory work. Hence we can understand why the college-preparatory work has had and still has a strong influence in determining the scope and aims of the work of secondary schools and in the distribution of the emphasis on the various phases of that work whatever the social or economic condition or the future educational aims of their pupils, taken all together, might or may be.

What I have been saying in somewhat labored terms is this. Because our secondary schools originated as college-preparatory schools, and because college-preparatory pupils were then and always will be of the leading classes, or at least of those classes that aspire to intellectual or social leadership, or both, it is and was inevitable that the kind of education preferred by the social and intellectual élite was and is considered just good enough by ambitious parents who could or can send their children to the high school.

Now, the ambition to achieve distinction through self-improvement is a val-

SECONDARY EDUCATION

uable asset to the individual and to society. We welcome it whenever it appears. But it gradually became apparent that that ambition could not be realized by way of the college-preparatory work for those pupils who could not go on to college — always the great majority. It was clearly seen, as time went on, that the college-preparatory work, if not followed by college education, was unsatisfactory for most pupils as preparation for a progressively significant career, — such a career as that at which those pupils or their parents aimed, — or for fuller enjoyment of the serious pleasures of life, or as a stimulus to further education. In time, therefore, it was realized both within and without the teaching profession that the value of college-preparatory training for most non-collegiate pupils was, and still is, greatly overestimated.

In estimating the value of the classical

course in our secondary schools, thoughtful people took into account not only what the pupils could get out of it, but also what they had no opportunity to get. What they got was a more or less satisfactory elementary acquaintance with the elements of the Latin and Greek languages, and a very rudimentary acquaintance with small portions of the literatures of those languages, together with the elements of algebra and geometry, some ancient history, and very little else. What they had no opportunity to get may be described as follows. The classical course left the pupil eighteen or nineteen years old untouched by the beauties, the solace, and the inspiration of the literature of his mother tongue, and without the power to speak and write English with something approaching accuracy and ease; it gave him no training in history and government that would enable him to under-

SECONDARY EDUCATION

stand and appreciate the institutional life of organized society, including our own; it gave him no training in natural science, and so left him without the power to understand or appreciate some of the most important thought and activities of his time; it gave him no training in a modern language that would open to him the intellectual resources and the genius of other modern nations; it gave him no training that would enable him to understand and appreciate to some extent the art treasures of his own and of all time; it afforded no manual training that might give him, by way of laboratory experience, an understanding of the industrial activities whereby society keeps itself going; it provided no opportunity for vocational training; it afforded no opportunity for self-discovery except for the pupil of linguistic or mathematical ability; and, lastly, it had paid no attention to his physical development and vigor, on which all his usefulness and happiness ultimately depend. Such a course, whatever it might be as preparation for a college course that might make good the omissions and defects of the earlier course, could not, in general, conduce to intellectual superiority or social leadership. Contemporary needs were not provided for in it save incidentally and remotely.

I have said that the difference between what secondary-school pupils got and could not get was realized in time by the teachers and the thoughtful public. The literature, lay and professional, of the eighteen-eighties and nineties is replete with discussions of this important issue. I shall not attempt to name individuals who were most influential through this literature and in other ways in bringing our secondary schools to the point of actually making the changes seen to be necessary, although some of them were

SECONDARY EDUCATION

very influential indeed. But however great their influence was, as individuals, they could not effect the desired reforms save in a very limited way. It was only when they organized for the cause they advocated, that the needed improvements in secondary education began to be made in earnest and over a wide area.

I shall therefore restrict myself to reminding you of the fruitful work — work that conspicuously yielded practical results — done by agencies consisting of individuals *working together*, in regional associations of teachers and in the National Education Association.

These agencies were (and are) the New England Association of Colleges and Secondary Schools; the Committee of Ten on Secondary School Studies, and the Committee on College Entrance Requirements of the National Education Association; the North Central Association of Colleges and Secondary Schools;

the College Entrance Examination Board (emanating from the Association of Colleges and Secondary Schools of the Middle States and Maryland, although the original suggestion leading to its establishment came from New England); and the Commission on the Reorganization of Secondary Education of the National Education Association.

I single out these agencies for special mention because of their outstanding achievements. In so doing, I do not intend to minimize the help rendered by other associations of college and secondary-school teachers, associations of superintendents of schools, and regional and national associations of departmental teachers — teachers of English, history, and the rest. Moreover, all these agencies deserve mention for another reason. They represent that method of voluntary coöperation for the solution of educational problems to which I re-

SECONDARY EDUCATION 13

ferred a moment ago. Associations of teachers for the consideration of educational questions are, of course, common the world over. But, abroad, when important questions of educational policy are to be dealt with, representatives of the teaching profession are called together by the government; and the government ultimately decides on the scope and content of the report to be issued. With us, although the teaching profession has no such professional standing as it has on the continent of Europe, the teachers themselves voluntarily undertake to solve the problems of educational reform. The agencies I have mentioned illustrate voluntary cooperation on a large scale. Happily this procedure has become established among us. It has not always been as fruitful as in the instances of which I am about to remind you; and it remains to be exercised in ways not yet tried, as I shall point out later. But we have it, and may justly expect it to serve us well in the future.

When the public high schools sought to modify the scope and nature of their work in response to the broader community demands as well as college-preparatory demands, difficulty was experienced in meeting both sets of demands in most schools — the larger as well as the smaller, though naturally the difficulty was greater in the latter. Bearing in mind the established preëminence of the traditional college-preparatory work and the conception of it as the conventionally correct thing, it was inevitable that conflict should develop between the claims of the college-preparatory work and the other work — both demanded by the public — on the time and energy of the school.

The satisfactory adjustment of these two sets of demands was a difficult pro-

SECONDARY EDUCATION

cess and a long one. Indeed, the end is not yet; but much progress has been made. This adjustment, difficult in itself, was aggravated by the differences between the admission requirements of different colleges. These differences were not limited to subjects of study but included also differences in the subjects themselves. The latter were sometimes so great that schools could not meet the admission requirements in certain subjects for different colleges without maintaining parallel courses in those subjects, and this, of course, made inordinate and unnecessary demands on the schools.

The necessity of attacking this problem of adjustment effectively became acute during the last two decades of the last century. It became more and more apparent that something more than talking and writing must be done to bring about the desired result. *Action* was needed — action by agreement between the two parties most affected by the controversy.

Then appeared the important coöperating agencies I have mentioned. The first of these was the New England Association of Colleges and Secondary Schools, — significantly calling itself at first the New England Association of Colleges and Preparatory Schools, and retaining that name until 1915, — which came into existence in 1885-86.

The most important achievement of this Association was to bring home to the colleges, which at that time tended to maintain an attitude of authoritative direction toward the secondary schools, the plight of the schools — especially of the public high schools — when they tried to satisfy the varied demands of the colleges and also the broader demands of their communities. It promoted important modifications in college-admission requirements which eliminated some of the most unreasonable differences between the requirements of different colleges. It also influenced favorably the enlargement of the scope of the admission requirements; that is, it helped forward the trend toward accepting a wider range of subjects as suitable for college-admission purposes. These achievements tended to enable the schools to give more nearly adequate attention to the newer subjects — a much needed consummation.

The enlargement of the scope of the college admission requirements was not, however, for some time, as has already been intimated, an unmixed advantage. The traditional college-admission requirements quite generally remained in force; they were, indeed, strengthened. Owing to the time-consuming character of those studies and persistent collegiate preference for them, it happened that the newer studies were frequently treated in stepmotherly fashion, and so failed to satisfy the desires of the schools, of the public, and of the colleges. It was the day of scrappy courses in all except the traditional studies; that is, the time allotted to the newer studies was inadequate, and there was little continuity or intensiveness in the pursuit of them once they had been undertaken. There were also great differences in the achievements of the schools in the traditional studies. Indeed it is not too much to say that secondary-school programs of study the country over varied so greatly that the program situation could almost be described as chaotic. Additional difficulties were experienced in effecting a satisfactory articulation of elementary and secondary schools, and in attempting to do well in four years all the work that should be done in the high school — four years being at the time the almost universal length of the secondary-school "course."

SECONDARY EDUCATION

The problems involved were of national importance. So it was natural that the National Education Association should take a hand in the endeavor to solve them. The National Council of Education (a department of the National Education Association) made a signal contribution to their solution by appointing a Committee on Secondary School Studies—the famous Committee of Ten. That Committee made its report in 1893.

Besides its valuable report, the work of that Committee gave new and significant evidence of the value of the principle of voluntary coöperation in the solution of educational problems. The Committee (itself consisting of school and college teachers) appointed nine conferences, each of ten members similarly selected, to consider, severally, the time limits, the best methods of teaching, the most desirable time allotment, and the best methods of testing the pupils' attainments in the nine principal studies at that time recognized as appropriate secondary-school studies.

The reports of the conferences proved to be a significant contribution toward a more promising solution of the problems submitted to the conferences than had been theretofore achieved. Further, inasmuch as several of the conferences desired an earlier beginning for the studies they had under consideration, — that is, an earlier beginning than the ninth school year (the first high-school year), pointing out the well-nigh impossible task of doing adequately in only four years what ought to be accomplished by secondary-school pupils — in view of these facts, the conferences considered and caused the Committee of Ten to consider, the wisdom of a new and better articulation of elementary and secondary education, namely, the

SECONDARY EDUCATION

extension downward of the period of secondary education. The Committee of Ten adopted the suggestions of the conferences, and thus foreshadowed the advent of the junior high school, although the junior high school did not actually appear in our public-school systems until about twenty years later.

Two immediate results of the work of the Committee of Ten apart from those just mentioned were also of great importance. The first of these was the formulation of four sample programs of study for four-year secondary schools based on the recommendations of the conferences. Although in the estimation of the Committee those programs should have been considered as mere scaffolding for the construction of actual programs, they were widely used as they stood, or nearly so. Nevertheless, those programs accomplished much in bringing order into the chaotic state of secondary-school programs of study. The other result was a reënforcement of the not yet fully established conception of the public secondary school as primarily a school that must meet the needs of a majority of the community, and only incidentally a college-preparatory school. This reënforcement appeared in the report of the Committee, in no uncertain terms. The report says:

The secondary schools of the United States, taken as a whole, do not exist for the purpose of preparing boys and girls for colleges. . . . Their main function is to prepare for the duties of life that small proportion of all the children in the country — a proportion small in number, but very important to the welfare of the nation — who show themselves able to profit by an education to the eighteenth year, and whose parents are able to support them while they remain so long at school.

In order that any successful graduate of a good secondary school should be free to present himself at the gates of the college or scientific school of his choice, it is necessary that the

SECONDARY EDUCATION

colleges and scientific schools of the country should accept for admission to appropriate courses of their instruction the attainments of any youth who has passed creditably through a good secondary-school course, no matter to what group of subjects he may have mainly devoted himself in the secondary school.

And the Committee adds that this is not possible because of the unsatisfactory condition of secondary-school programs of study. That was in 1893.

In 1895, on the initiative of the Department of Secondary Education, that Department and the Department of Higher Education of the National Education Association, together, appointed a Committee on College Entrance Requirements. That Committee made its report in 1899. It traversed again some of the ground covered by the report of the Committee of Ten, and in similar fashion; and some of its recommendations repeat, though in somewhat stronger terms, recommendations of the earlier Committee. Notable among these were the recommendations that any study among those dealt with by the Committee on College Entrance Requirements, if pursued with a sufficient time allotment, should be allowed by the colleges to count toward admission to college; and a more emphatic statement of the recommendation of the Committee of Ten concerning the reorganization of the seventh, eighth, and ninth school years of the public-school system as a junior high school, although the name "junior high school" was not used.

Two other recommendations of the Committee on College Entrance Requirements were influential in promoting progress in secondary education. One of these, and the one that had the most immediate influence, was that secondary schools should establish "national norms," or units of work (a unit mean-

SECONDARY EDUCATION 25

ing a year's work with substantially the same time allotment in a given subject), so that these units of work would have substantially the same meaning throughout the country, and might therefore be accepted by any college toward satisfying its admission requirements. The other recommendation was that teachers in secondary schools should have acquired a college education or its equivalent. (Technical training for secondary-school teachers — professional training — received no mention.)

By 1900, so much progress had been made toward defining the scope of secondary education as a whole, and in the definition of national units of work in the studies at that time established in secondary schools and recognized by the colleges as suitable for college-admission purposes, that a new coöperative agency was seen to be possible for maintaining and improving the standards (quantity and quality of work) in secondary-school studies that had been attained, at least on paper, and, in no small degree, in practice, during the years that had elapsed since the founding of the New England Association of Colleges and Secondary Schools in 1885. This new agency was (and is) the College Entrance Examination Board, consisting, once more, of college teachers and secondary-school teachers and deriving all its functions from those two groups of teachers, working together. As is well known, the Board sets uniform examinations for admission to college throughout the country; the examination questions are formulated and the results of the examinations graded by representatives of the school and college departments concerned. In spite of some mistakes made by the Board and, on occasion, perhaps, because of no little adverse criticism of it, acceptance of the work of the College

SECONDARY EDUCATION 27

Entrance Examination Board has become nation-wide, there being few if any colleges that now depend on their own examinations in preference to those of the Board.

Of all the regional associations, none has surpassed the achievements of the North Central Association of Colleges and Secondary Schools in promulgating and enforcing contemporary standards in the "accredited schools" of the Association — and only such schools can become and remain members of the Association. The Association standards cover not only standards for secondary-school studies, but much more that is of great importance to the life and work of a satisfactory school; as may be seen from the following brief outline of the standards for 1925. They are ten in number: (1) buildings — their location, construction, equipment, and care; (2) adequate library and laboratory facilities; (3) approved records of scholarship and attendance; (4) requirements for graduation — fifteen units of work, not less than thirty-six weeks in the school year; forty minutes (net) minimum length of time for a recitation; (5) efficiency of the instruction and spirit of the school — determined by inspection; (6) salaries — must be such as to enable the school to obtain and to hold teachers possessing the qualifications demanded by the Association; (7) preparation of secondary-school teachers (of academic subjects)—equivalent to graduation from a college belonging to the North Central Association, which must include a minimum of eleven semester hours (after 1925, fifteen semester hours) of the study of education; (8) the teaching load — some factors conditioning the efficiency of the instruction — the following are recommended as norms: (1) pupil-teachers ratio, 25 to 1; (2)

SECONDARY EDUCATION

number of classes per teacher, daily, 5; (3) daily class enrollment per teacher, 150; (4) number of students per class, 25. . . . "An average attendance in excess of thirty pupils per teacher, or more than one hundred and sixty pupil hours, or more than six periods per day for any teacher, shall be considered a violation of this standard " — (double periods may, under certain circumstances, be counted equivalent to one class-room exercise); (9) the pupil load — in general, four unit courses per pupil; only pupils ranking in the highest 25 per cent of the class may take more; (10) program of studies — "the Association recommends that three units in English, two units in Social Science, one unit in Biological Science or one unit in General Science, and one unit in Physical Education or Health, with or without credit, be required" for graduation by all "four-year" high schools. It further recommends the introduction of vocational subjects, such as agriculture, manual training, household economics, and commercial subjects, into schools where local conditions render such introduction feasible." A sufficient number of qualified teachers must be provided. "Not less than the equivalent of the full teaching time of three teachers may be given to academic subjects."

Another achievement of the North Central Association should be noted in passing. This is its success in enforcing standards for colleges as well as for secondary schools, and thus influencing favorably the education of college graduates who become teachers in schools accredited by the Association. It will be remembered that only such graduates or persons having an equivalent education may teach in such schools. Further, as early as 1903, the Association reaffirmed the democratic conception of

SECONDARY EDUCATION

secondary education that had been set forth by many individuals and had found recognition in the organized agencies working for the improvement of secondary education that I have already mentioned; and all the work of the Association has been in harmony with that conception ever since.

During the past ten years the National Education Association has again rendered important service to secondary education through its Commission on the Reorganization of Secondary Education. That Commission, taking into account all that had been done by its predecessors whether individuals or associations, once more defined the "objectives" of secondary education in its own words, and made important new contributions in defining the objectives of the several departments of secondary-school work. The work of the Commission has been widely influential in promoting general acceptance throughout the country of the reorganization of our public secondary schools from the old plan into the junior-senior high school scheme of organization.

Though both these results of the work of the Commission are important, the latter deserves more emphasis than I have yet given it. The junior-senior high school scheme, in spite of many shortcomings, may fairly be characterized as the most promising educational agency yet devised for the discovery of the capacities and needs of individuals and the progressive planning of their education from the seventh school year onward in the light of that discovery. The junior-senior high school organization thus marks an important advance in the endeavor to plan the secondary education of every individual in the light of individual and social needs; that is, in the light of the purpose for which our public schools exist.

SECONDARY EDUCATION

What the future may bring forth in the matter of extending our public secondary education upward so as to include the junior college, cannot be predicted. But the present trend certainly points that way. If the junior college should become an integral part of our public-school system, I am persuaded that we should round out our public secondary education with great profit to our whole educational endeavor, and our best pupils would, moreover, be in a better position to accomplish results comparable to the best achievements of continental secondary-school pupils. The continental secondary schools, as is well known, carry their work about two years beyond our secondary-school work; but that is accomplished by the time their students are no older than our present secondary-school graduates. Whether we can save those two apparently lost years by means of the junior college is a question not now answerable.

All workers in the field of secondary education have been greatly aided by the literature in their field which came into existence, in this country, about 1890 and developed rapidly in quantity and quality. Before the eighteen-nineties educational periodicals dealt with the undifferentiated field of education. In the early nineties appeared successively two periodicals — "The Academy," and "School and College" — both devoted chiefly to secondary education and both decidedly creditable publications. Each of those journals lived only a short time. But they were followed immediately by the "School Review," which soon became, as it is now, the leading periodical in its field in this country (and it does not suffer by comparison with similar journals wherever published). During the nineties,

SECONDARY EDUCATION

also, books dealing partly or wholly with secondary education began to appear. To-day the annual output of books and articles dealing with secondary education is large.

During the past thirty-five years, and particularly during the last dozen years or so, another agency has played an increasingly important part in promoting the improvement of secondary education, namely, the college and university departments, or schools, of education. They have sent out a host of teachers with an educational insight and outlook — a professional consciousness — not formerly attainable by beginners in their profession and promising much for the future. They have not all nor always maintained the standards of general, nor indeed of professional, scholarship that should be maintained. But they have already rendered good service and we may justly expect much more from them in the future. The teachers they have sent out are at work on the firing line — in the secondary schools where such standards as we need must be applied and reforms must be adopted in spite of all sorts of practical difficulties. Moreover, in and through those schools of education research in the field of secondary education has made its appearance and is being energetically promoted. Slowly but surely we have come to regard research in education, as we regard research in all other human endeavor, as indispensable to progress.

One other important agency in helping to provide our contemporary opportunity in secondary education must not be overlooked. At least one of the great foundations, — the General Education Board, — among its other great and numerous gifts to education, has stimulated the establishment of public secondary schools throughout the South by

SECONDARY EDUCATION

grants in aid of local taxation, and by paying the salaries of professors of secondary education in southern colleges. Without this help many communities in the South now supporting public high schools might still be without them.

Looking carefully at our secondary education as it is, we see that the result of all our striving since the seventeenth century, is, at its best, a great opportunity; and it is a considerable opportunity, even when that best is only approximated. At its best, this opportunity may be described as follows: We have a junior-senior high school that is a refining and unifying force in our complex society — a school that, in spite of many shortcomings and the often weak reënforcement its best endeavors win from the general public, offers the elements of general culture to all normal children approximately twelve to eighteen years old who are led to seek general culture through the persuasive influence of a good beginning at an early age. At the same time, it provides more and more satisfactory opportunities for the pupil to find himself, and to make the most of his dominant interests and powers as he proceeds. It provides for the pupil early in his secondary-school career preliminary vocational training and experience, and later, actual vocational training if he wants it. Accompanying these opportunities for general culture and for vocational training, this junior-senior high school provides continuous educational and vocational guidance, so that the danger of inappropriate education of the individual pupil may be minimized. A flexible scheme of classification is provided whereby pupils of approximately the same ability are taught together, so that each will feel the stimulus of measuring himself with his peers and have a

SECONDARY EDUCATION

chance to proceed as fast and as thoroughly as he can, or as slowly as he must. During the whole secondary-school period the school guards and promotes the pupil's health and physical development by theoretical instruction and directed physical exercises. Through its curriculum and its management it provides for the development of character, that is, of moral ideals and conduct in harmony therewith; and with the same end in view, it encourages and helps to carry on a great variety of collateral or extra-curricular pupil activities. This school is well articulated with the elementary school on the one hand, and with the college on the other. It is open to all children of the community, without tuition, on precisely the same terms. This is our public secondary school at its best. We have also endowed and private schools, notably some schools carried on in connection with university departments or schools of education, which are organized on the same general plans as the public junior-senior high school.[1]

Taking the secondary schools the country over, or in a single state, to what extent do they really afford the opportunity sketched above? *We do not know.* Nor do we know what they actually accomplish with whatever opportunity they do afford. All that we do know is that the opportunities afforded by our secondary schools vary greatly, and that their product — the secondary-school graduates — is a very uneven product as to scholarship, character, and all the other qualities essential to superior citizenship. This statement is based on general experience and observation during a long period of time — in my case, more than forty years.

[1] They, too, like our best public schools, are contributing, each in its own way, interesting further insight into the problems of secondary education and to the progressive solution of those problems.

SECONDARY EDUCATION

Is it not time that our secondary schools were studied seriously, with a view to finding out just what their status really is, and just what their accomplishments are? I am aware that "measurement" is now in vogue in the high school as well as in the elementary school; and that is good as far as it goes, although, for various reasons, it has not made as much progress in secondary education as in elementary education. But I mean something else — something that should precede, or, at least, accompany the use of intelligence tests or achievement tests. I mean, first of all, a study to determine to what extent our secondary schools afford the opportunity that has been sketched as the best, and to what extent they approximate it. Such knowledge is necessarily antecedent to measurement of the details of accomplishment; for accomplishment can be judged fairly only in the light of opportunity. Since it is impossible, at present, for any one agency to measure the thousands of secondary schools of the country in this way, could one or more of the regional associations of colleges and secondary schools, perhaps with the coöperation of the state department or departments of education (or of one of the great foundations), be induced to measure, say fifty to a hundred schools lying within a given area; the schools to be so chosen as to be representative of the secondary schools of the region? And may we not cherish the reasonable hope that, in case of need, a number of schools varying greatly in opportunity would voluntarily offer themselves for such measurement?

Suppose for this measurement, the standards of the North Central Association of Colleges and Secondary Schools were used, to begin with. Those standards are certainly not unreasonable for any self-respecting secondary school.

SECONDARY EDUCATION

Possibly those standards could be combined in an index number, and the results of applying this measure to the chosen secondary schools made widely known. Such results could, of course, be published without mentioning a single school by name, although each school would naturally wish to know the results so far as they apply to that school. The working out of such an index number and volunteer effort in using it might challenge, it seems to me, the interest and coöperation of schools of education, if their assistance were desired, as probably it would be.

Individual schools and the schools of a region or of a state would be, after such measurement as has been suggested, in a position to appraise justly the results expected of them in view of the conditions under which their work was done; and, in case of need could take steps to remedy deficiencies in those conditions or achievements on the basis of ascertained facts. It is well known that facts and only facts convincingly set forth will move the teachers and the powers that be to remedy defects that cry out for remedy. Whatever the defects of such an index number as I have suggested may be, I am confident that the use of it would show facts enough to help mightily toward improvement of the conditions under which many of our secondary schools now carry on their work, and improvement of the results they accomplish.

Meanwhile, whether the suggestion just made is thought fruitful or feasible, I offer the following. Why not launch a determined concerted effort toward making the most of the potential scholarship found in every secondary school — to bring it to as high a stage of development as is possible under the limitations of time for secondary education and

SECONDARY EDUCATION

the maturity of secondary-school pupils? As to maturity, I cannot refrain, in passing, from expressing the conviction that our secondary-school youth are intellectually as immature as they seem to be because, in general, we have not challenged their powers as we might, with advantage, challenge them. No doubt, if we continue to treat a secondary-school youth as if he were still a child, he will remain a child. But if he has a chance to realize that more is possible for him and that more is expected of him than is possible for or is expected of a child, he will tend to respond accordingly.

A moment ago I asserted that the quality of our secondary-school graduates varies greatly in the matter of scholarship. It is not too much to say, I think, that secondary-school (and, incidentally) college graduates are, with notable exceptions, characterized by intellectual flabbiness instead of intellectual vigor. Intellectual interests make only a mild appeal to them or no appeal at all. We — school teachers and college professors — all affirm that scholarship is a precious thing; but too often we tolerate indifference to it or lukewarm devotion to it. Although a modicum of scholarship is demanded for admission to almost every career, and real preparation for the professions is based on it, we do not refuse to accept indifferent scholarship as preparation for college and for the professional schools to the disadvantage of both — which is general disadvantage.

What is needed is a *militant attitude in favor of scholarship* — a serious intellectual purpose that is pervasive, insistent, and indomitable. This attitude must be developed, if at all, by secondary schools and colleges. We are here primarily concerned with the appearance and dissemination of that attitude by

SECONDARY EDUCATION

secondary schools, that is to say by the secondary-school teachers. How may they make progress in that direction?

The first step might be something like this. Every secondary school should be alert to recognize its superior pupils whether they happen to be preparing for college or not; should study them with care, segregate them and see that they have every opportunity to delve as deeply and to travel as far beyond the average pupils as their superior ability enables them to go. I know that something like this is done here and there. What we need to do at once is to make special provision for the superior pupils universal; or at least to make such provision in all save the small schools. If such procedure is once firmly established in the large schools, a way will be found to provide by transfer of pupils to larger schools, or otherwise, for superior pupils whose local schools are too small to afford adequately the special attention to which such pupils are entitled. Of course, teachers have always been interested in their gifted pupils. They could not help it. But those pupils have only occasionally received the special attention to which that interest ought to have led. My contention is that *to care for the superior pupil in a manner befitting his superiority is an imperative duty.* But to discharge this duty effectively will once more require concerted action on the part of secondary-school teachers locally, regionally, and nationally. To take steps to secure such concerted action might well enlist the active interest at least of local and regional associations of secondary-school and college teachers.

Further to ensure recognition of and emphasis on scholarship among the pupils requires corresponding emphasis on scholarship among the teachers. To

SECONDARY EDUCATION

that end a fair proportion of secondary-school teachers should be persons of superior scholarship — this superiority to be attested not merely by scholarly distinctions won during the teachers' careers as students in college or university, good as such distinctions are in constituting a presumption of scholarly habits. But whether the individual who has won those distinctions really has strong and persistent intellectual interests can only be determined by later experience. A permanent scholarly attitude and habits in conformity therewith are attested only by growth in scholarship as time goes on. Is it too much to expect that every good-sized secondary school shall have on its staff teachers who are also productive scholars? Such teachers are common in continental secondary schools. With us they are rare. Without more of them we shall hardly attain that aggressive attitude in favor of scholarship in our secondary schools to which I have referred.

Suppose, now, that some local or regional association of secondary-school teachers or the National Education Association should seriously undertake a campaign for — to begin with — only a small proportion, say five to ten per cent of real scholars in the teaching staffs of our larger secondary schools. Suppose a feature of this campaign were to secure higher salaries for such teachers than the regular salary schedule provides; and appropriate increases of the salaries of such teachers as long as they continue to give evidence of scholarly habits, provided they are also good teachers; suppose further, that this campaign explained clearly the wisdom of assigning such teachers chiefly to the gifted pupils as suggested above. If some such campaign were undertaken and pushed energetically, secondary-

SECONDARY EDUCATION 51

school teachers would prove that they are as much interested in the scholarship aim as they are in the other important aims of the school. At present we have no collective evidence on this point.

Preceding or accompanying such a campaign, is it not possible and desirable for strong secondary schools to take some such stand for scholarship as has been outlined? And would not such a stand on their part tend to leaven the whole lump? Is it not the plain duty of our secondary schools to move in this direction?

Of course scholarship is not the sole aim of secondary education in this country. For most of our secondary-school youth we must be content with conscientious endeavor — under duress, if necessary — to learn what they are able to learn with varying degrees of enthusiasm. For the inclusive aim of secondary education in this country, for all pupils at whatever stage their school life may stop, is to lift the general level of our prospective citizens in health, knowledge, power, character, vocational efficiency, and political judgment, whatever the native ability of individuals may be, above the level possible for elementary education; *to do this so as to make the most of every grade of ability including the highest.*

Perhaps one reason why so many of our pupils are not keen about intellectual interests is that we have tried, more or less consciously, to make them all attempt the achievement that is fairly easy for the few. Failing to bring the mediocre pupils — the great majority — up to the achievements of the gifted we have compromised with scholarship. But shall we continue to do this? Shall we not rather, while doing all we can to secure the maximum achievement of which the rank and file are capable,

SECONDARY EDUCATION 53

also challenge the capacity of the gifted pupils by expecting of them more and better work than can be done by the rank and file? And would not they and society gain greatly thereby?

There is an agency ready to hand that we have not employed as we might to promote progress in secondary education. I mean the alumni associations, especially the high school alumni associations. So far as I know such associations have rarely represented anything more than loyalty — rather vague but genuine — to their schools and good fellowship. Loyalty and good fellowship are decidedly worth while, but it seems to me they are not now utilized as they might be.

Suppose that a high-school alumni association, under the unofficial but effective leadership of the principal and his staff became actively interested in the following questions: What opportunities does our high school afford? How do those opportunities compare with the opportunities afforded by other high schools similarly circumstanced? Does our school make adequate provision for the gifted pupils? Are the accomplishments of our school commensurate with its opportunities? Suppose those questions were kept uppermost in the minds of the alumni by two fairly large committees consisting of members of the association and reporting to the association at least once a year, say at the annual meeting. Could not a secondary-school alumni association, under the leadership suggested, with the information such leadership might supply, be counted on, through the influence of enlightened public opinion, as a real asset for progressive educational advance to an extent not hitherto realized?

A few words about foreign secondary schools. It is difficult to appraise justly

SECONDARY EDUCATION

our accomplishment in secondary education in comparison with foreign accomplishment because of the very different conception of secondary education and the equally different conditions under which it is carried on here and abroad. In European countries secondary education is class education. It is not tuition free, and hence is beyond the reach of most young people of secondary-school age. The pupils, on the continent, are almost completely homogeneous, and elsewhere fairly so, in respect to race and nationality and social or economic status. Their parents are generally socially and economically above the wage-earning class, and have subscribed to traditions of culture (including scholarship) for from one to many generations; and even when this background is absent they know that secondary education is the *sine qua non* of admission to preparation for a career or to a career itself

— as distinguished from a wage-earning occupation — especially on the continent. Moreover, the period of secondary education usually covers the years from the pupil's ninth or tenth year to his eighteenth or nineteenth year of age.

Foreign secondary-school pupils with such an origin, living in such an environment, and with such incentives are very differently situated from the majority of our secondary-school youth. Accordingly, it does not seem profitable to attempt any broad generalizations concerning the accomplishment of foreign secondary education as compared with our own. It is profitable, however, to dwell on some details.

From what has been said, it is obvious that the foreign secondary school, especially on the continent, can count on the reënforcement of the homes, particularly in the matter of scholarship to a degree quite impossible in this country. While

SECONDARY EDUCATION

in Great Britain respect for scholarship is not so marked as on the continent, the importance of scholarship is acknowledged, as it is in this country. But the *dominant* aim of the British secondary school is strongly supported by public opinion, within and without the school. That aim is to imbue every secondary-school youth with the best traditions of British manhood and citizenship — independence in thought, initiative in conduct, sincere devotion to British standards in national and international affairs, unswerving honesty and imperturbable courage in public and private life. How great an asset this aim together with the public opinion behind it is can hardly be over-estimated; for, it is not merely an aim to which everyone subscribes, it is a vital force permeating the school in every detail of its life.

To be sure, a similar aim is cherished in our secondary schools. But because it cannot count on a pervasive and unequivocal public opinion comparable to that in Great Britain, it is far from influencing our secondary-school pupils as the corresponding aim influences the British pupils.

European secondary schools possess another advantage over ours — in the scholarship of the teachers, especially on the continent. In Germany or France, it would be impossible to find secondary-school teachers who have had only four years of secondary education followed by normal-school education (or their equivalent); and in Great Britain such secondary-school teachers are rare. With us they are common. A few teachers in our leading endowed and private schools and in our leading public schools can claim a closer approximation to the scholarship of their European colleagues than teachers in the country at large. But even such schools cannot claim as a

SECONDARY EDUCATION 59

class the scholarship possessed by the teachers in corresponding continental schools. Under the circumstances, it is inevitable that continental secondary-school graduates should surpass our own in scholarship; and that British secondary-school graduates should show superiority over our graduates in certain personal qualities.

If foreign secondary-school standards were unreasonably high, and permanently beyond our reach, our present secondary-school inferiority in respect to certain standards of opportunity and accomplishment would not disturb us. We know that they are not too high; nor can we admit that they are beyond our reach. Voluntary and conscious inferiority of opportunity and accomplishment is not only discreditable, but tends to lower the level of our citizenship below that of the corresponding citizenship of European countries. Our responsibility, therefore, is plain.

60 SECONDARY EDUCATION

At its best, we have achieved a real opportunity in secondary education for our youth of both sexes. We are as yet far from realizing this opportunity save in favored communities. How to make this opportunity more general, and progressively more responsive to our needs, and how to make accomplishment more and more commensurate with opportunity is still as it has been our secondary-school problem. It cannot be solved all at once nor once for all. Its solution offers a perennial challenge.